RAINMAKING
101
FROM DAY 1
Workbook

Packaging, Positioning, and Pitching
EXPOSED

Precious L. Williams

Publishing Services by: Pen Legacy, LLC.
Cover Design by: Christian Cuan
Edited & Formatting by: Carla Dean, U Can Mark My Word

Library of Congress Cataloguing – in- Publication Data has been applied for.

ISBN: 979-8-9872891-6-7

PRINTED IN THE UNITED STATES OF AMERICA.

First Edition

Other Works by Precious L. Williams

Bad Bitches and Power Pitches: For Women Entrepreneurs and Speakers Only (2019)

Bad Bitches and Power Pitches: The Workbook (2020)

Pitching for Profit: The Bad Bitches Playbook to Convert Conversations into Currency (2021)

The Pitch Queen: A Women's Journey from Poverty to Purpose and Profits! (2022)

Books can be purchased at Amazon.com, Barnes & Noble, Walmart.com, BAM! Books a Million, and PenLegacy.com, or get your autographed copies from my websites:

Perfect Pitches by Precious
www.perfectpitchesbyprecious.com

and

Perfect Pitch Group
www.perfectpitchgroup.com

Table of Contents

RAINMAKING 101 FROM DAY 1 Workbook

Packaging, Positioning, and Pitching
EXPOSED

DEDICATION

To those ready to embark on their greatest adventure in life, discovering who you are and unleashing all of you on this world, remember these two ALWAYS:

Fortune favors the bold!

Dream BIG, Ask BIGGER!

Introduction

What you are holding in your hands right now is your ticket to real power in your profession. I am NOT being dramatic. This book gives you the secret to building clientele, being a sought-after expert for media, and building the type of relationships that will provide you entry into a world not seen by most attorneys. How? Through the power of Rainmaking!

What I Thought Being a Big-Time Attorney Was vs. What It Is

I remember May 25, 2007, like it was yesterday. I graduated from Rutgers Law School with my family and friends in attendance. I captured a dream that many times seemed impossible, passed the New York State Bar on my first try, and thought my life was set! I became a newly admitted young attorney, eager to put that work in and show myself as talented in the courtroom as well as outside of it. On top of that, I was an associate at a prestigious Top NY law firm! What could go wrong? Everything!

Precious L. Williams

The #TRUETEA on Firm Life as an Associate

You see, I did not know the game of the legal industry and profession. I was an outsider stepping into a brand-new home who did not understand the rules of engagement. I was excited to work and become the next Perry Mason or Johnnie Cochran. I also dreamt of conquering the media with my fresh legal take on the biggest case of the day/week. Big dreams! However, I knew nothing about the concept of Rainmaking. I often heard the term in law school and at events but never understood it.

Now that I am a successful serial entrepreneur, I understand what was missing when I started practicing. I needed a completely different mentality! The truth is society has prepared us to be worker bees and keep our heads down. But it's time to EXPOSE the #TRUETEA. The worker bee mentality is not going to cut it. Not now or ever! Leaving the worker bee mentality behind, I had to become the Queen Bee. I needed to be a Rainmaker.

Being a Rainmaker is essential to attracting, building relationships, and gaining new clients. Only then would I or any lawyer have real power in the legal profession. Being a Rainmaker gives you the ability to command top dollar in the marketplace.

Worker Bee No More

Many of us have been taught the worker bee mentality as young attorneys and professionals, but we all MUST know that being able to sell and secure clientele is the REAL name of the game. That is why I want to introduce you to Rainmaking 101, my associate friends. I will share what law school professors, mentors, or the Old Boy's Network would never teach you.

Rainmaking 101 From Day 1

Throughout this book, I'm going to share how to be a Rainmaker so that you unlock unlimited opportunities. Let's GO!

The Definition of a Rainmaker

What is a Rainmaker? A Rainmaker is any person who brings clients, money, business, or even intangible prestige to an organization based solely on their associations and contacts. The Rainmaker is usually regarded highly by other employees within the company and is a key figure like a principal, partner, or executive. The term is sometimes used in the context of political fundraising, as well.

Key Takeaways

- A Rainmaker is a person who brings clients, business, and money to their firm.
- A retired politician with a large following and the ability to raise campaign funds for others is also a Rainmaker.
- The term is often used in the legal profession and business, investment banking, and entertainment.
- Technically, a Rainmaker can exist in any part of any business.
- An individual who brings real, positive change to an organization is a Rainmaker.

Understanding Rainmakers

Traditionally, the term "Rainmaker" has been applied to members of the legal profession, such as politicians with law degrees who retire from public life to practice at nationally recognized law firms. However, over time, the term has gained usage in many other industries and activities, including investment banking, political campaigning, and public speaking.

Ref.: Rainmaker: Definition, Traits, How to Become One (investopedia.com)

This book will be divided into the 3 P's: Packaging, Positioning, and Pitching. Now that I've traveled the world, have become the #KillerPitchMaster, and have entered boardrooms and training facilities that only a few are invited inside, you need all three to be a real Rainmaker!

PACKAGING

Making It Rain

The Power of Rainmaking

Let me be brutally honest and clear. Being a Rainmaker is NOT for the faint at heart. Your ability to secure clients (and ultimately top-tier clients) puts the ball in your court. Rainmaking, quite simply, is POWER. You already know you are at a law firm to make more money than they currently pay you. It is assumed you can do the work, or you would not be there. However, in lean times, Rainmaking is crucial. Your ability to build lasting relationships in different realms means you have a consistent and steady Rolodex of connections that can become clients.

What Is a Book of Business?

According to The Balance, "A book of business is the list of clients maintained by someone who provides specialized professional services, such as legal and financial services."

Ideally, the professional regularly adds clients and customers to keep their book of business growing.

Precious L. Williams

Professionals who might keep a book of business include:

- Lawyers
- Financial advisors
- Private and investment bankers
- Financial planners
- Certified public accountants (CPAs)
- Insurance sales agents
- Salespeople

How Does a Book of Business Work?

Your book of business should include all customers or clients you have worked with in the past. As you acquire a new client, add them and their information to your book of business. Your book of business is ideally ever-changing and evolving, with new information added about your clients as your relationship progresses.

[As an attorney], maintaining a healthy book of business means keeping in touch with existing customers and clients as you cultivate new ones so you're front and center in their minds when they again have a need you can fill.

Your book should be more than just a list of names with corresponding telephone numbers and contact information. A comprehensive book includes details of each transaction and other data, even personal tidbits. Other items to include are:

- Demographics, such as age and occupation
- Revenue generated from the client
- Referrals, if any
- Potential future needs

Developing and maintaining relationships is a key function of your book of business. Since networking is about building relationships, it's a good skill to possess when building a book of business. You can network the old-fashioned way through networking events and other in-person functions. You can also grow your network through social media, marketing, and branding.

Valuating a Book of Business

Your book of business has monetary value because the clients within it (and your relationships with them) represent your past, current, and future income. Additionally, each client may potentially connect you with a referral, thereby growing your client list and business.

Depending on your industry, you can define your book's value by the revenues each client contributes to your coffers monthly or yearly. For example, a financial advisor at a given firm might have a book of business that includes one hundred clients and $100 million in client financial assets.

It offers a measure of personal satisfaction to know what your book of business is worth—mainly as it grows—and it's not uncommon in some industries to sell your book to another practitioner. Such a transaction is most common in investment, law, and insurance circles. You sell your leads when the time comes that your book is no longer useful to you, such as when you retire or if you change careers.

Do I Need a Book of Business [as an Associate]?

To grow your business as a professional, you need a way to organize your clients, keep up to speed on their needs, and identify future growth paths for your business. Keeping a detailed and frequently updated book of business is a proven method to achieve these goals.

Ref.: <u>Book of Business: What Is It? (thebalancemoney.com)</u>

Why Does It Matter Right Now to Start Thinking Strategically about This?

From the very first day you start at a firm, you should begin observing who the power players are, aka The Rainmakers. Seek them, know them, watch them, and find a way to emulate them so you can be them. If you don't become a power player, you will be presumed to be a worker bee. If you listen to conventional wisdom, you will think working hard is all that matters. NEWSFLASH! #TrueTea! Worker bees are a DIME A DOZEN. Worker bees can be replaced at any time. Rainmakers, Queen Bees, and King Bees are always needed because they bring clients, goodwill, and respect to the firm. So, from here on out, think about the power and tap into your beginner Rainmaking Power from Day 1. If you keep reading this book, I will show you how!

The True Lies of Networking

The truth is that most people dislike networking because it feels inauthentic. They think they must have a canned pitch, and since most pitches sound the same, nothing is really gained. I'm going to help you shift your mindset about networking and pitching. But first, I want you to understand that your ideal prospects are not everywhere or at every event.

This is why packaging yourself will help you get clear about where you should be.

You do not have to attend every legal event, bar reception, attorney networking event, or business meet and greet to become a successful Rainmaker. If you do that, you waste your time with all the wrong people, and we all know time is precious. You do not need to be everywhere with everybody—especially when they are not your people. Wasting time is NOT a great way to become a Rainmaker! Finding the right people, positioning yourself, and getting known for what you do is.

The Power of Now

Listen, I get it. With all you have on your plate, why not put this off? I mean, you are probably new to your firm, getting yourself acclimated to the culture, or don't fully appreciate what it means to be on the partnership track. So why pursue becoming a Rainmaker now? Because those who start early set the pace for their career. While others are focused on doing great work, your goal as a Rainmaker is to begin the process of gaining clients and packaging yourself to position yourself for greatness. Listen, great work is essential. However, sales, gaining clients, getting known for what you do, being seen in the media, and getting referrals from those who like, know, and trust you will put you in a much higher sought-after place. Trust me; no one gets rid of successful Rainmakers. Partners and power players will keep you with their firm much longer and fight for you to stay. In contrast, worker bees just get replaced! Period!

Precious L. Williams

Rainmaking Is Your Second Job

Yes, you read that right! Rainmaking is your second job! Your payday might not come for a while, but it will be powerful and lucrative when it does. Building relationships takes time. Sales can take time. Gaining clients' trust and loyalty takes time. But if you do it right, that first client may lead to many others. Isn't this what you want? The time will pass anyway. So, use your time wisely! #TRUETEA

GET KNOWN FOR WHAT YOU DO

The truth is that until you show up, no one knows you. Hiding behind a computer screen tells me nothing about YOU! The social media version that no one has ever met — let alone talked to — is killing many young associates. Now is the time to show up in a way that matters. No, it's not about the number of events you attend. It's about bringing yourself to quality people so you can develop the type of relationships that turn conversations into currency and, subsequently, more clients. So, let's dig in and get this work!

The following are step-by-step tips to get your ideal clients to like, know, trust, and vouch for you. To become a Rainmaker in your firm, you must do great work and get known for what you do—online and offline. To get known for what you do, the following are my hard and fast rules you must follow—starting now!

1. **Social Media**

   Be strategic about how you show up in online searches. If you've never done this, search for your name on social media and assess the results. What words are used? Are

24

you coming across as an expert or a lurker with no staying power? Do a social media audit on Facebook, LinkedIn, Twitter, Instagram, Clubhouse, and TikTok. Write down the results of what was said and/or written about you. Did anything surprise you?

2. **Build Your Social Media Presence**

   Now that you have the results from your research, it's time to become strategic about how you show up on Facebook, LinkedIn, Twitter, Instagram, Clubhouse, and TikTok. Be mindful of who you are connected to. As you build your Rainmaker presence, make a note of who you should be connected to. Be intentional about why you should be connected to anyone you identify. As you look over the Top 1-3 social media platforms, make an assessment of your network. Are you connected to people you know? If not, why? And let's not get into vanity metrics such as "likes" and comments that will never convert.

3. **Building Up Your Rainmaking Presence**

   How do you describe yourself on social media? What is particularly attractive in your bio or explains what you do with specificity? Is it accurate, or does it reflect who you used to be? If your description needs to be updated, decide what is missing. Take it a step further and share your bio and other online profiles with a few trusted individuals. What is their opinion? #TrueTea, you may be showing up as a professional, but your words might not be connecting to your ideal clients. To build a Rainmaking presence, you must be seen as a relatable expert who understands the needs and wants of your ideal client. Accordingly, make sure whatever you post reflects your true personality and does not make you seem bland.

4. **Get Known as a Power Player at Your Firm**

   Who do YOU need to know you? Get them to want to know YOU. Study them; watch what they say and do around certain people. You may learn that the people with the "names" are not the most powerful at your firm. That is why you must stay in the know and master emotional intelligence. When others want to argue their point of view, sit back and observe. Once you see who has the real power, it's time to introduce yourself in a way that matters. Do your own investigation by asking associates, paralegals, and long-time secretaries about your firm's Rainmakers. Find out the Rainmakers' wants, needs, desires…and proclivities. Stay in contact with them on a bi-weekly or monthly basis. Seek what they need and make yourself available. Keep them updated on what you are working on inside and outside the firm or have coming up. Share the cool things you are doing outside the firm.

5. **Create a List of Trusted Individuals**

   Do you have a personal list of trusted individuals who could serve as valuable, income-producing power players? If so, do you know their wants, needs, and desires? More importantly, do they know what you do? If not, it's time to educate them. Make a list of these people, and create a list of the most important things you want them to know about you. Share with them your goals and dreams. Ask them how they view you. Get ready to be surprised in a good way! Make them aware of opportunities that they can refer you to others. Ask them who they know that may need your help. This is part of packaging yourself and educating others on how to pitch you. Create a message for them to share, whether via text or email.

6. **Identify Individuals Who Will Vouch for You**
   Build an online presence of people who will recommend and vouch for you. It's time to get strategic in how you move from now on.

7. **What Do Each of These Say About You?**
   You must know what your network already says about you. The truth is most people know you on a surface level. However, when opportunities arise, that surface-level knowledge will keep others from automatically referring you and your services to family, friends, or a trusted network. They will not even consider you an option. That is why how you are packaged matters. How you teach people to pitch you when opportunities present themselves and you are not around is critical. Go deeper! You are building up your Rainmaking presence.

Without knowing any of these, you are setting yourself up for failure. Most attorneys are ignorant of what it takes to build relationships and, ultimately, clientele and referrals. Don't let this be you! Start with a Rainmaking mentality from Day 1.

Precious L. Williams

THE PITCH GAME

As the Pitch Queen, it is vital we do foundational work. This requires you to understand the fundamentals of PITCHING, SELLING, AND CONNECTING WITH OTHERS ON A REAL LEVEL! Oh yes, we are going there!

1. What Is a Pitch, and Why Is It Important to Rainmaking?
2. How to Set Up Your Ideal Prospects to Become Your Clients
3. How to Make Your Clients Referral Sources in the Future
4. The Preparation Work Needed to Build Your Credibility (so when they look you up, you are solid online and offline)

In your own words, describe what a pitch is. Why is it important in Rainmaking?

How long is a pitch generally? Where are some places you can pitch to your ideal audience?

_____

_____

_____

_____

_____

_____

Who is your best target market for pitching? Why? Demographics? Psychographics? Why should they choose you?

_____

_____

_____

_____

_____

_____

_____

Where can a Rainmaking pitch take you in your career and life? THINK BIG!

_____

_____

_____

_____

_____

_____

_____

_____

_____

_____

_____

_____

_____

_____

_____

Precious L. Williams

Why is it important to YOU to become a Rainmaker? What are your main goals?

_____

_____

_____

_____

_____

_____

_____

_____

_____

_____

_____

_____

_____

_____

_____

_____

POSITIONING

Authentic Relationship Building

Are you ready to go ham and cheese on 'em? Ready to set yourself apart from those who think technology is the ONLY way to make it in your career as an attorney? If so, let's go!

1. **Building Relationships in an Era of Transactional Relationships**

   In this society, everyone is being told to get what they can from others and keep people at a distance. The #TRUETEA is that transactional, tit-for-tat relationships will get you nowhere. Building authentic relationships will. Everything does not always pay off initially, but when I tell you that the riches, wealth, and clientele are so much sweeter over time, they are! See if you have chemistry with someone first instead of trying to get something in the beginning. Meet people online and offline, for coffee, at events, and check in with them. THIS IS WHAT MAKES A DIFFERENCE! Human beings need to connect in real life and virtually, so make the encounter memorable and a true experience. Clients, customers, and referrals flow from that. Play the long game, not the transitional game.

2. Meeting 1:1

Listen, I understand. You don't have all the time in the world. But can you spare 10-15 minutes for a virtual call? How about 15-30 minutes to meet with someone over coffee or tea? Make the time to show up at an event so they can interact with you in person. In an era of technology where texts are prioritized over calls, be the difference people can measure. Yes, you can marry old school and new school! Just care about others, too, but not in a Pollyanna way. Sure, some people will fall off, and some relationships may never come to fruition. But the ones that do? #Priceless!

3. Meeting at Networking Events

a. How do you make these networking events work for you?
If you can, check out who will be there ahead of time and resolve to meet 3-5 quality people, NOT EVERYONE!

b. What to do after the networking event to make it worthwhile?
Of course, the fortune is in the follow up. However, I want to encourage you to do something a bit

more. If you come across something that's in their industry, send it to them in a link in an email or message. This shows that you are thinking of them. Awards and honors they may want to go out for but don't know about? Get curious about them and they will get more curious about you!

YOUR BRAND IDENTITY

What is your personal brand, and what does your legal brand represent? What do you stand for? If someone mentions your name, what do you hope they say about you when you are not present? Again, developing a personal brand identity is key. You want to create a positive and influential narrative about you and your brand. This is not easy and takes care and precision. Before people want to become your client and the firm's client, you must build trust and a stellar reputation and have others vouch for you. You can do this in several ways:

a. **Loyalty**

   Have you shown loyalty to others while they were successful or when they fell? Did you offer encouragement and words of faith and positivity? It's time to demonstrate the same to your clients. As you build your clientele, these people will always vouch for you.

b. **Authenticity**

   Are you showing up how you think others want to see you or are you moving as your authentic self? Start asking trusted individuals what they see in YOU. It may surprise you what they say. You may find out you have always had their support but didn't know it because you never asked for help. When they share what they see in you and how you show up, it becomes a part of your brand story. Your authenticity will go up because they see the real you. This may help you see that you are not showing up as they know you to be, yet they still see you!

c. **Transparency**

Are you known for telling tall tales (lies) or giving the truth in love, even if blunt? Can you be trusted to tell the truth? If you do not have a squeaky-clean past, do you acknowledge your mistakes, and have you worked to overcome them? Does it bother you to talk about it, or can you share from a place of healing and transforming others?

d. **Storytelling to Different Audiences**

Everyone has a story. Some have feel-good stories; some have sob stories. But the best stories are the ones you can share at the right time, depending on the occasion. Wherever you are on your journey, start from a place of power before telling the not-so-pretty parts of your story. At networking events, retreats, or while seated next to someone on a plane, try out different stories and see how they resonate with others. We all have stories that will unite us with others who have experienced heartache, heartbreak, lost love, career pivots, first job loss, and blessings birthed from mistakes.

RAINMAKING BUSINESS DEVELOPMENT

What is Rainmaking business development? Sales and gaining new clients! Now that we have gone through all this beforehand, it's time to take REAL action. To some, this is just a numbers game. To me, this is also a strategic game. The right connections sometimes come from the most ordinary situations. They say in order to make friends, you must first be a friend. If no one is reaching out to you, start reaching out to others genuinely.

1. **Reach Out**

   Take the first step and reach out to people in your network and others who are winning. Let them know you care. What's new in their world? Reach out without asking for anything, even if they expect it. Keep them guessing. Your job is to reach out to five people every week via text, email, or phone call. And keep up this schedule!

2. **Learn About Others Beforehand**

   Find out their birthdays, family life and relationship status, likes, and dislikes. Tap the tea leaves, and get the word on the street. This will show initiative and impress others that you took the time in advance to make them feel important.

3. **Know Your Craft and Personality and How to Use Them to Your Advantage**

   Have you ever been told you are too much or felt out of place? Guess what? We all have. A few short years ago, I decided to be totally me. No code-switching. I give all of me unapologetically. That's when others started to say they saw me. They felt me. I was no longer a robot. I was human! Funny, self-deprecating, the life of the party. I used to let gatekeepers hold me back, but that got nowhere fast. However, when I allowed myself to become my most authentic self, I started showing up colorful, bold, and professional in all my full-figured glory! Why don't you give that a chance? Be you!

4. **Know Your Firm's Power Players Who Can Vouch for You**

   Most people see their firm's big-name partners and associates and run for the hills. I get it. Interacting with those in a more powerful position can be intimidating. But I encourage you to observe them as humans and go beyond the surface level. Look around at your firm's events and see who has the juice. Work on your pitch. Read about your firm's power players and their list of dream clients. Tap into the "word on the street/#truetea" at the office. Feel comfortable sharing what you are working on or would like to work on. Also, share your hobbies and fun things you like to do and what you learned they like to do. Approaching power players with confidence shows you have done your homework and will impress them.

KNOWING WHO YOUR IDEAL PROSPECTS ARE

The truth is there are prospects everywhere! The difference is knowing who the right ones are for you. This is why you should niche down—so your efforts are targeted. When you begin the process of niching down, you will start to see how much fun it is to pitch. With the right prospects, it's like hitting a bullseye each time. That way, your prospects will know you are speaking to them and have what they need. Everyone else won't matter until you are successful in that niche. Capiche?

1. **Testing**

   Testing is trying different positioning and pitch tactics. Are you more women or men heavy in your network? Are you targeting organizations? If so, which types, professions, etc.? With testing, you will see in real-time which approach works better. When sending a phone call, text, email, or social media post, take note of who responds more to what you put out. Also, assess how your audience responds. Is it with enthusiasm, likes, comments, or following up with a message to know more?

2. **Research**

   Trust me when I say research is not dead. Your local business library is helpful in this regard. They have access to surveys and other business information you can access for free with your library card. You may even be able to do this from home. A librarian can help you learn what's popping and where your industry is going. By knowing these things, you will have a pulse on hot topics you can speak about, as well as what the experts say about what is coming up. Imagine having all this info and data in your arsenal. You will be unstoppable! Find the business library in your area and make an appointment. Get a library card. Access the different business and law databases. Get help from the librarian. Doing so will help you focus on your efforts and produce results.

3. **Who Is Naturally Drawn to You?**
   Have you ever looked at your network to see what types of people engage with you the most? At networking events? In real life? Family members and/or friend groups? Start paying attention to who they are and to who they are connected. Remember, strategy is like what GI Joe said—"Knowing is half the battle!" What you do next with this information is how you #slayallcompetition.

4. **Who Are You Naturally Drawn To?**
   Are you connecting more with corporate types, creatives, nonconformists, etc.? Men, women, children? Why? Seriously ask yourself why that is. This is a question to examine deeply because it will show you something about yourself. It may even reveal a new audience or industry you never thought about and no one else is taking advantage of. Don't miss out!

DEVELOPING A LUCRATIVE NETWORK

During your Rainmaker 101 journey, building and sustaining a lucrative network is crucial. Your network—consisting of future clients, referrals, and opportunities— becomes a funnel for you and your firm. In this section, we will focus on creating a real-life Rolodex.

As with many things in life, and regarding this workbook,

eat the meat and spit out the bones. If it doesn't fly, don't apply. This workbook will grow with you!

1. **Volunteer Your Services**

    When I say volunteer, I mean in ways that match your schedule, hobbies, interests, and causes. As you seek volunteer opportunities, consider where you will find your best prospects. Are they only at exclusive events or support certain causes you can get behind? While volunteering in that organization, stay focused on who you need to know and WHO NEEDS TO KNOW YOU!

2. **Develop a Relationship Through 1:1 Meetings**

    Whether for lunch, coffee, or virtually, you are building rapport with each other. You are not asking for anything. You are seeing if you both have mutual good chemistry. Make a list of people you would like to meet with for 15–30 minutes live or virtually. What will you discuss that is easy-breezy, yet you still learn about each other?

3. **Participate in Networking Group Activities**

    Get involved in group activities you want to learn. These activities may include golfing, rowing, sailing, house tours, walking tours, historical tours, etc. You can also create your own opportunities and events to meet others and establish your brand. The world is your oyster!

    You can find networking activities on the following platforms:

1. LinkedIn (www.linkedin.com)
2. Meetup (https://www.meetup.com/)

4. **Attend Charitable Fundraisers/Silent Auctions**

Attending charitable fundraisers and silent auctions helps you move in circles with high-net-worth individuals. These events cost more than the average because of the quality of attendees. THESE ARE WORTH IT TO BUILD YOUR BOOK OF BUSINESS! The first to four-year time period is crucial to you. These events are not for the general public, so choose wisely. Who is attending that you want to meet? What silent auction item do you have your eye on? As you walk around, strike up a conversation with others.

5. **Become the Go-to Resource at Your Alma Matter**

Building or rebuilding a relationship with your college or university is essential. Circle back and get to know who's who in administration now. Send updates on yourself so it can be featured in the alumnae/alumni magazine or on social media. Remember, you are building your social media profile. Also, take an interest in your other alumnae/alumni who are popping. Reach out and congratulate them. Let them know you are both alums and show your support. Flattery works, but genuine flattery with strategy is #killer!

PITCHING

Pitching To Different Audiences Creates a Pipeline of Ideal Prospects

As you build your lucrative network, getting your name out there in other ways is also important to create a buzz and draw prospects to you. How? Let's take this discussion about pitching into overdrive!

1. **Media**

   Have you ever wondered why some attorneys are featured so much in the media (TV, magazines, streaming services, newspapers, and online sources)? They have made a name for themselves in that space, so the media keeps calling on them. You have access to this type of exposure, too. Your practice area needs a fresh voice like yours. As you grow in your legal career, make a list of hyperlocal, local, regional, national, and even international media where you would love to be featured. What are you great at speaking about in your industry? Let's get that pitch together! You now have another audience who SEES YOU AS AN EXPERT!

2. **Investors**

   Even though you are NOT seeking investors for the firm, remember that investors hang with high-net-worth individuals, entrepreneurs, and CEOs. And what do they all need? Legal representation! See how we did that? So, check out business pitch competitions and angel investor events—live and virtual. Start seeing which investors are in the room and why. What companies are they interested in giving coins to? Make a note! How does this apply to your law practice? All of this will help you create a great sales pitch as you build relationships with investors.

3. **Referrals**

   Have you ever asked people in your network to refer clients to you or promote your services to others? How about wanting them to invite you to network events with their well-connected friends and associates? We all live busy lives, so make it easy for your network to refer people to you. Also, educate your network on what you do and your ideal clientele. They may only know one side of you. Give them more so they can trust you, feel you are human, and genuinely care to help you network.

4. **Elevator Pitches at Networking Events**

   Have you ever been to a networking event and heard attorneys introduce themselves? It can be quite boring, and you probably wish you were watching paint dry instead. Don't let this be you. Time to turn up the heat! This is your time to shine. Let's get that elevator pitch together so you can captivate and titillate in thirty seconds to one minute.

SPEAK YOUR WAY TO SUCCESS

Public or professional speaking opens doors to lucrative opportunities, clients, and referrals. We know most people fear public speaking. When you are the speaker, people focus on you. They look for you to guide, instruct, and be the expert. Imagine having your prospects right in front of you while you confirm what they are thinking or offer a fresh, unique perspective. Speaking makes you the ONLY choice that matters!

1. **Speaking: Why It Matters**

   Learning how to speak well publicly is CRUCIAL. Imagine having a captive audience as you enlighten them about your field of law. Imagine speaking to an audience your firm partners cannot. Imagine making a name for yourself by speaking. The speaking world is not oversaturated when it comes to legal issues and being able to speak to those issues in laymen's terms. Since most professionals do not utilize speaking as a lead generation source, you are already ahead of the game. Use your craft of being able to speak about it in elementary terms and kill the game. You'll be seen as an expert, and the clients will come. Period!

2. **Speaker Types and Options**

   You can take advantage of many types of speaking engagements, and not all the audiences have to be legal professionals. You can be a keynote speaker, speak at workshops and non-legal events, and do presentations at breakout sessions for conferences and summits. Imagine your funnel full of clients because you went in other directions and even in different industries than the rest! Cha-ching!

3. **Make Sure If You Are Speaking, Your Network Knows It**

   You know what that means, right? It means you are to post about where you are speaking. Share the flyer and link to check out the event details. Invite your friends to tell their friends. Encourage them to email and text their network. If you are more of a transactional attorney, find speaking engagements in other states. Speaking builds your brand, and building your brand catches the eye of partners. The #TRUETEA is that your law firm partners are power players who truly understand business development and will be checking on you. Initiative pays off!

4. **Make Sure You Publicize Your Speaking Engagement Both Before and After**

   Publicizing your speaking engagement brings credibility and much-needed visibility to you and your brand. Prospects love to see where professionals like yourself are speaking so they can attend. By doing so, you also prove to them that you are getting out there. With your posts, you are getting new eyes on yourself. They will take notice. After the engagement, post pictures of you speaking to and interacting with attendees. If possible, get on-the-spot testimonials. The photos and testimonials can be added as content that you can use over and over again to promote your brand and silence the doubt.

a. **Different Industries**

Want to know how to keep them guessing and tuning in? Look for non-obvious places to speak to share the depth of your talent. Yes, speaking engagements lead to clientele and customers. It also attracts conference organizers and event planners and presents them with transferable topics that could change their industry. These opportunities bring you before others who may have never heard you speak. Blow them away! Period!

b. **Establishing Yourself as the Expert**

Speaking gives you instant credibility. All eyes are on you while the attendees listen to every word you say. With that kind of respect, you must show up as the expert! You must project confidence and remain open. Speaking is a muscle that you must repeatedly use to get better. It is different from being in the courtroom. As the expert, people want to learn something different from you than what everyone else is saying on the topic. Breathe new life into your subject matter and become the go-to person in your field and other fields based on your topic.

Precious L. Williams

WRITING YOUR WAY TO SUCCESS

Oh, you thought posting on social media, attending various events, and doing speaking engagements were the only ways to get out there? No! Writing is a great way to establish credibility and visibility and gain clientele! How sway!

How to Slay All Competition with Your Pen Game!

1. **Show Off Your Expertise by Getting Your Fresh Perspective Out There**

    Do you have a unique way of explaining legal matters to everyday people? Or can you relate pop culture to legal issues? Start writing about it! Post on your social media, contribute to other people's blogs and newsletters, etc. Make use of your LinkedIn and social media accounts. The right titles, topics, and posts can go viral on the right networks. So, get to writing!

2. **Speaking Engagements Will Follow**

    As you write and gain traction, it will lead to webinars and even requests for you to do live speaking events. Trust me; writing is essential to turning your prospects into clientele and customers.

3. **Create Your Own Blog**

    Let me tell you, I still read blogs—short, medium, and long! Write a blog on a topic you are interested in exploring. Your blog can be about your favorite hobby, challenging the status quo, or sharing more about yourself and what you are discovering about life, love, your career, etc. People love to see how others think. Give them something to talk about!

4. **Write Interesting Thoughts and Write Often**
   In the beginning, you are learning your rhythm. So, every day, jot down in your phone or journal ideas you want to explore. This will become a list of several ideas you can explore over time. Try to stick to topics that are relevant to what is happening in the world at the time when you are blogging.

STRATEGIC NURTURING AND FOLLOW UP

After going through much of this workbook, you may be at a loss of whom to reach out to and may even be scared. You may feel you are disturbing others. Banish these thoughts from your head! You want to be a Rainmaker, right? Then you must develop a system to connect, follow up, and serve your ideal clients. Ask for meetings, request 15-minute phone calls, and suggest discussions over coffee or tea. Most importantly, show up. The more you ask now, the less you will have to do later. Dream BIG, Ask BIGGER!

Here are some places to start to find your prospects:

1. College or law school (classmates, professors, staff, and administration)
2. Prior employment or current workspaces (team members, co-workers, and superiors)
3. Charities, volunteerism, board positions
4. People connected to your family or children
5. Sports events

6. Temples, churches, mosques, and places of worship
7. VIPs you have come across in everyday life
8. LinkedIn for research and updates (Look up and connect with people you admire or have worked with before.)
9. Facebook
10. Instagram
11. Twitter
12. TikTok
13. Clubhouse
14. Facebook Groups (Do not spam!)

#PITCHPLEASE
The Elements of a Basic Pitch

Who are you?

_____

_____

_____

_____

_____

_____

_____

_____

_____

_____

_____

_____

_____

Precious L. Williams

What do you do?

_____

_____

_____

_____

_____

_____

_____

What specific legal problems/challenges does your law firm handle?

_____

_____

_____

_____

_____

_____

_____

_____

What is your specific industry? Who are your ideal clients?

_____

_____

_____

_____

_____

_____

What "secret sauce" difference maker do you offer in addition to your firm?

_____

_____

_____

_____

_____

_____

_____

Precious L. Williams

What happens next if the prospect wants to work with you?

_____

_____

_____

_____

_____

_____

_____

_____

_____

_____

_____

_____

_____

_____

_____

_____

_____

Create an attention-grabbing hook or powerful call to action (CTA) that represents you and your firm well.

_____

_____

_____

_____

_____

_____

_____

_____

_____

_____

_____

_____

_____

_____

_____

_____

_____

Precious L. Williams

Based on what I have explained, create your basic pitch.

_____

_____

_____

_____

_____

_____

_____

_____

_____

_____

_____

_____

_____

_____

_____

_____

_____

_____

_____

Now write three additional variations of your pitch.

Basic Pitch #2

_____

_____

_____

_____

_____

_____

_____

_____

_____

_____

_____

_____

_____

_____

_____

_____

_____

Precious L. Williams

Basic Pitch #3

_____

_____

_____

_____

_____

_____

_____

_____

_____

_____

_____

_____

_____

_____

_____

_____

_____

Creating a
"Killer" Rainmaking Pitch

Now that you have learned the BASICS, have you:

1. Practiced it out loud?
2. In front of others?
3. Gotten feedback?

Do you feel more comfortable? Good! Now I want to introduce more advanced concepts to you to set your "killer" pitch on fire! READY? Great! Let's get started.

3 Ways to Build Your Confidence to Pitch

- Visualize yourself as you want to be and hold that image firm in your mind. Who and what do you want to be? Be as specific as possible.

_____

_____

_____

_____

_____

_____

_____

_____

Precious L. Williams

_____

_____

_____

_____

_____

_____

_____

_____

_____

_____

_____

_____

_____

_____

_____

_____

_____

- **Affirm yourself daily. How are you speaking to yourself? What top ten affirmations will you COMMIT to telling yourself every morning and night?**

_____

_____

_____

_____

_____

_____

_____

_____

_____

_____

_____

_____

_____

_____

_____

_____

Precious L. Williams

- **Do one thing that scares you every day! Continually doing this creates the momentum that can trump all FEAR! What have you been afraid to try? Write and break down your most pressing dreams and COMMIT to taking a scary step daily!**

Precious L. Williams

It's time to take your *PITCH* to the next level! Have you ever heard a pitch that took your breath away? In this next section, I will teach you how to "kill it" in your pitches in several unique ways. To create a "killer" pitch, start here!

Pain Points

A great pitch starts by addressing your target market's pain points in their own words, not yours. Knowing what truly keeps them up at night and articulating your pitch with confidence will save you time and time again. Sometimes, pain points may not be addressed because some people might not know they exist or believe there is a solution.

1. What is your target market struggling with in their business and/or personal life? How do you know? Have you asked them?
2. Have you done your research? What research have you done? Have you gone to the library and looked up actual data? Does the data support what you want to put out to the world?
3. Does your pitch reflect what your target market needs to hear now?
4. Are you offering a real solution? If so, put it in the pitch with clarity!

Purpose

What is the purpose of your pitch? What are you hoping to accomplish? Being very clear in your purpose can help create a great pitch. Know why you are pitching in the first place. Why are you doing this? Why are you the ultimate resource/solution?

Is it to:

1. Gain the first client or more clients? If so, why?
2. Warm and nurture new prospects? If so, why?
3. Become an industry leader? If so, why?
4. Create more content that attracts your ideal audience? If so, why?
5. Establish your expertise in the industry? If so, why?
6. To entice, captivate, and titillate the media? If so, why?
7. Secure paid and free speaking engagements? If so, why?

NOW…

Start working backward from your purpose. Begin with the end in mind.

Precious L. Williams

What would you want to know about your firm's legal services if someone else were pitching it to you?

_____

_____

_____

_____

_____

_____

_____

_____

_____

_____

_____

_____

_____

_____

_____

Know Your Audience

Most attorneys THINK they know their audience and how best to serve them. In my opinion, they are almost always WRONG! Why? Because most times, they have not done the research or due diligence to understand their audience. This is a critical step that must be taken seriously!

Ask yourself the following questions:

1. Who is your ideal target market or prospect? Why? Demographics? Psychographics?
2. What is your competitive advantage over everyone else?
3. How do you measure up to what your competitors are offering?
4. Are you neglecting a particular demographic?
5. Do you think too BIG?
6. Are you thinking too small?
7. Why do you want to speak to this audience or industry?
8. What gap is not being served right now that you can exploit?

Master Your Story

Being an expert storyteller is vital in any pitch. Stories illustrate your main points as you pitch or speak. Have you ever considered what stories define different aspects and areas of your life?

- o What inspired you to become an attorney?
- o What life stories make you cry?
- o What most shocked you on your journey to becoming an attorney? (Let's refer to this story as "behind-the-scenes" tea.)
- o What are some of the challenges you have faced and overcome?
- o What life experiences do you still struggle with and are making some headway with now?
- o Common traps?
- o The reality of associate life?
- o What excites you about your profession?
- o What do you add that is different in terms of perspective?

Precious L. Williams

- o Which of your stories apply to your Rainmaker business mission and purpose? List them!

Why are stories important in pitching? As children, we learn through hearing stories. Those stories stick with us and connect us with others. Make sure your story is emotionally compelling, relatable, and makes you appear more human and less salesy. Some story ideas include:

- o Sharing why you chose your firm over other firms.
- o Stating what gap(s) you saw in the market that you knew you could fill.
- o Answering the question of who your firm services.

Passion

Passion is the glue that holds your pitch together. It is the fire, energy, and intensity that will instantly attract others to you. It is your "why" taken to the next level. Express your passion every time you pitch! Why?

- o It is contagious.
- o It makes others see who you really are.
- o It helps you stand out.

Precious L. Williams

Share your why. What is your reason for doing what you do?

_____

_____

_____

_____

_____

_____

_____

_____

_____

_____

_____

_____

_____

_____

_____

_____

Precious L. Williams

Keep asking yourself why five times in a row until you feel the true emotion. This is more for you and not your prospects. It keeps you in check.

Practice Makes Perfect

Practice, practice, practice! The best pitch means nothing if it does not roll effortlessly off your tongue. That is why each of the preceding steps is important. They are the catalyst to make sure you take pitching seriously!

- o In what ways will you COMMIT to practicing your pitch?
- o Will this be daily? If so, how many times daily?
- o What prep work do you need to do?
- o Who is someone you can practice in front of and who is committed to helping you get better? Why?

Final Thoughts

The end is actually the beginning…

Now that you have read this book and completed the exercises, do you see how Packaging, Positioning, and Pitching are crucial to your Rainmaking journey? Refer to this book time and time again while progressing in your career. As you grow, some of these chapters may apply at a specific time than others. Keep coming back to this book with fresh eyes. The truth is your Rainmaking journey has just begun! I am proud to walk beside you, reminding you of your greatness every step of the way now and in the future.

The worker bee mentality is GONE! In its place…

Be the Rainmaker.

Be the King Bee.

Be the Queen Bee.

Your future success starts now. Are you ready? Let's go!

Here's to winning each day, one day at a time! The world is yours!

Acknowledgements

Thank you, **INROADS**, for providing me with my very first internship as a teenager in St. Louis, Missouri. I was an intern at Y/98 FM, an amazing radio station, and that gave me a taste for what I do today on the grandest stages around the world!

Thank you, **Junior Achievement**, for teaching me how to sell with confidence in my teenage years—the $500 Sales Club from way back! Now, I slay all competition in sales pitching and sales scripting for the Top Fortune 500 companies TODAY!

Thank you, **Spelman College**, for teaching me how to DREAM BIGGER than my reality and providing me with the tools to introduce all of me to the world.

Thank you, **Rutgers Law School**, for giving me a second chance at law school and becoming the attorney I always wanted to be. Also, for bringing me back to teach 1L's and 2L's how to pitch themselves with ease in a crowded, tough job market. Thank you to the MSP Program through **Dean Cliff Dawkins and Dr. Lenore Pearson** for seeing me again with fresh eyes! Finally, thank you to my Queen in Career Services, **Wendi Taylor**, for always encouraging me through my law school experience and beyond. I love you all!

Thank you, **Bill Schroeder**, for blessing me with the gift of introducing me to **Associate Dean Fran Bouchoux** at Rutgers

Precious L. Williams

Law School, which led to my second chance at law school. I completed the mission on May 25, 2007, and passed the NY State Bar on my first try. Look at me now! You are a BIG reason why I wrote this book. The power of connections and who can vouch for you! Bill, you continue to bless me with your greatness, and I will never forget you and your impact on so many like me who needed a second chance to succeed!

Thank you, **Rich Rawson**, for donating the New Jersey Scholarship that paid for my law school career—tuition, fees, books, and bar review expenses. You got me to where I am today!

Thank you, **Savvy Ladies**, for showing me how to become an inspiration to others after hitting rock bottom. I came out of darkness swinging and received the Savvy Ladies Inspiration Award in 2020—two years after I walked out of homelessness. Dreams do come true! I went from award winner to now being on the Board of Savvy Ladies! If you find it in your heart, please donate to this wonderful organization that helps women by providing for them financial tools to help get them back on their feet after a job loss, during a transition, and to further their education. Thank you, **Stacy Francis**, **Judy Herbst**, and the Queen who helped me get the idea for this book off the ground, **Lisa Zeiderman, Esq.**! The website to donate to this non-profit is www.savvyladies.org.

Thank you, **Dress for Success Worldwide**, for providing clothes to me as I started interviewing while at the Bowery Mission Women's Center. I landed both prestigious positions looking the part. Since then, I have spoken at numerous DFS Conferences. I especially want to thank **Dr. Kimberly Iozzi** and **Natalie Borneo**. To donate to Dress for Success Worldwide, please visit their website at www.dressforsuccess.org.

Thank you, **Bottomless Closet, Executive Director Melissa Norden, and Program Manager Pam Kulnis,** for blessing me with my first speaking engagement in 2018-2019. You did not know I was a client at the time. Yet, I transformed what is possible for women like me. We are not done. We just need hope, your services, and support. To donate to this organization, please visit www.bottomlesscloset.org.

Thank you, **Toni Moore, Esq.,** for being a true inspiration to me as an attorney and a Queen who helped me by going through this book with a fine-tooth comb to make sure nothing was surface. Toni is the real deal! She reviewed my entertainment contracts and helped me navigate the world of media, and I trust her expert opinion. She has never let me down! #BAWSEMOVES

Precious L. Williams,
CEO of Perfect Pitches by Precious, LLC.
#KillerPitchMaster

Want to learn how to take your sales, investor, or elevator pitches from trash to straight CASH? Want your prospects throwing money at you every time you open your mouth? Then it's time to learn how to convert conversations into currency with the Pitch Queen, Precious L. Williams. Her company, Perfect Pitches by Precious (soon-to-be The Perfect Pitch Group), teaches you the tools and tenacity to pitch with power, sell with storytelling, and develop a masterful mindset for communication. Learn how to #SlayAllCompetition.

Bursting norms and shifting perspectives, Precious trains lawyers, law firms, and sales teams how to own their awesome and bring out their "WOW" factor. Your leaders and teams will up their game—on their terms—to develop the clarity and confidence that has been inside them all along. What's more, they'll get unstuck and discover a renewed and refreshed energy to own the mindset of the pitch in a way they never thought possible.

If you're ready to go from milquetoast to memorable, attracting and captivating your prospects while authentically closing the sale, it's time to #pitchforprofit. And you can bet you're going to have fun doing it!

Precious L. Williams is a 13-time national elevator pitch champion. She has also been featured on *Shark Tank*, CNBC, CNN, MSNBC, *Wall Street Journal*, *Forbes Magazine*, *Black Enterprise Magazine*, *Essence Magazine*, and the movie *LEAP*. Her clients include BMW, Microsoft, LinkedIn, Google, NBCUniversal, Federal Reserve Bank, Entrepreneur's Organization, Intuit QuickBooks, Yelp, Dress for Success Worldwide, Harvard University, and more. Precious is a dynamic international professional speaker, Top Fortune 500 corporate sales trainer, and 4X bestselling author.

Coming Soon From
The Perfect Pitch Group
www.perfectpitchgroup.com

The Perfect Pitch Academy

Rainmaking 101 from Day 1 Retreats and Training Programs (for Law Firms and Sales/Finance Professionals)

Online/Digital Pitch and Communication Skills Products

Precious L. Williams

Precious L. Williams

CPSIA information can be obtained
at www.ICGtesting.com
Printed in the USA
BVHW051438180423
662564BV00008B/567